MW00875915

A Beginners Guide to iOS 10 and iPhone 7 / 7 Plus

(For iPhone 5, iPhone 5s, and iPhone 5c, iPhone 6, iPhone 6+, iPhone 6s, iPhone 6s Plus, iPhone 7, and iPhone 7 Plus)

By Scott La Counte

Table of Contents

Introduction 4

Let's Begin! 5

The iPhone Crash Course 29

Surfing the Internet with Safari 35

Phone and Contacts 45

Taking Photos and Vidoes 50

Photo Editing 53

Photo Albums and Photo Sharing 55

Buying and Removing Apps 57

Siri 63

Messaging 65

Calendar 75

    Creating an Appointment 75

Security 77

Mail 78

Maps 79

Health 83

    Dashboard 83

    Health Data 83

    Sources 84

    Medical ID 84

Apple Stores 86

  iBooks 86

  App Store 87

  iTunes 88

Weather 91

Accessibility 93

    Zoom 93

    Text 93

    VoiceOver 94

Security 95

Touch ID..95

Encryption..96

Keychain..96

iCloud 97

Battery Tips..99

Essential Apps 101

Introduction

If you believe some news stories, the latest iPhone update (iOS 10) is radically different and you should beware of updating! They're wrong! This book is for both new users of iPhone and those upgrading to the latest update. I'll walk you through the changes and show you why updating is nothing to be afraid of.

The iPhone doesn't come with a handbook / user guide; this doesn't mean that you have to buy someone else's handbook! iPhone *does* have a handbook! There are three ways to get it:

1.   Download it from the Apple iBookstore (it's free)
2.   Get it online by going to https://support.apple.com/manuals/iphone
3.   Get it on your phone; if you go to your bookmarked pages on Safari, the last bookmark is for the 'iPhone User Guide'.

So why do you need this book? This book was written for my parents; people who needed to know as much as possible, as quickly as possible. There are people who want to know every single little detail about the iPhone, and you will find that in Apple's comprehensive manual. If you are like my parents though, new to the iPhone and just want to learn all the basics in about 30 to 60 minutes or an hour that is, then this guide will help you. People who just want to know how to add their contacts, how to take photos, and how to email.

It's not for advanced users, though if you are upgrading from the previous Apple iOS (iOS 9) then you will most probably find it useful.

If you are ready to learn read on!

Let's Begin!

iPhone is known for making radical changes in a way that is simple and easy to get adjusted to. So if you have heard that iOS 10 is a giant step forward, you need to realize to things:

1. It is!
2. There's very little learning curve

There are new gestures; new apps; and new menus—but most of the major changes are cosmetic changes…so the OS (Operating System) will a look little different, but largely behave the same.

The next section will include a crash course in using the device. Before I get to that, however, let's first look at some of the features you may have missed over the years.

From first look, the OS is very flat looking—turn the phone to an angle, and you'll see how much dimension there is to it—as you move it, it gently moves with you.

One of the biggest new features brought to users a few years ago in iOS 8 is the ability to get to virtually everything with one swipe. On your menu screen (when you first switch the phone on), there is no longer a bar to swipe.

On iOS 10, swiping gets you notifications, but to unlock the phone you need to press the Home button (hint: the only button on the front of your iPhone.

On older iOS menu screens (prior to iOS 8), you could swipe up the bottom right corner to quickly access the camera. You can still access the camera quickly, but you swipe to the right instead of the bottom.

You can also swipe up from any area of the bottom. This will bring up several options (including your camera)

The top bar has five round buttons:

- Airplane Mode – Switches cellular and wifi to off
- Wifi –toggles wifi on and off
- Bluetooth – toggles Bluetooth on and off
- Do not disturb – toggles on and off
- Auto rotate – toggles on and off

Below this is the brightness bar so you can quickly make your phone more or less bright.

AirDrop and AirPlay is next. AirPlay is an older feature that let connect your iPhone to Apple TV and AirPlay enabled devices (such as speakers); AirDrop is a newer feature—this lets you send photos and videos to people nearby who also have iPhones; it's a great (and easy) way to share photos.

The next row is newer feature (added in 2016) is "Night Shift." Night Shift let's you adjust the brightness and colors—the idea is to give you colors better on your eyes while you are reading in the night or early morning. You can even put it on a timer, so, for instance, it goes on everyday at 9PM.

The last (bottom) row has four buttons:

- Flashlight – one of the most popular apps on iPhone has always been flashlights (which use your phones camera flash and turns it into a flashlight); Apple has finally made the popular app one of their own by coming out with their own flashlight app and building it right into the main menu. Now you can quickly access the useful app anytime you need it.
- Timer – A long time iPhone app, this app lets you time what you're doing (such as cooking)
- Calculator

- Camera – You can access the camera in two different places; here and in the lower right corner.

In the past, you could play music from this menu. That's gone! But if you swipe to the right while you are on the menu, you'll see it's actually still here. It's just been moved over. This menu lets you skip / pause a song you might be listening to, as well as control the volume and what speaker it's playing on.

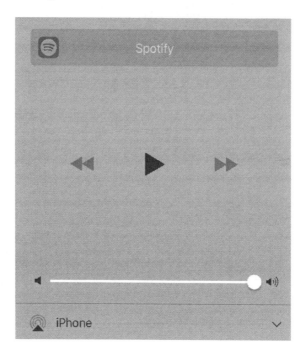

Also from the main menu screen, you can swipe down and see a number of different alerts (i.e. missed calls, email, text message, calendar, etc), which is called your phones "Notification Center." Your calendar is on the first tab "Today"; other apps that you have allowed alerts to will show up under the "All" tab.

iOS 9 added apps to your Today screen when you swipe down; so now you not only see your calendar and notifications, but you can see frequently used apps.

By default, the only thing that displays is battery life of active devices—watch and phone in the example above. But when you tap the "Edit" button, you will see a slew of other apps that you can add.

To add any app, tap the green plus button (and to remove any, tap the red minus button), and then tap done. After hitting done, your today screen will be automatically refreshed.

Remember, not all apps support this new screen; so if you aren't seeing an app, that doesn't mean it's not installed, necessarily—it just means it's not supported on this screen. It's a new feature, so while it may not be support now, it may be supported in the near future.

The swipe up from bottom and swipe down from top are two new gestures that work on all screens—even within apps. So anytime you are using an app, you can use these gestures to quickly adjust your sound, brightness, etc.

Previously (iOS 6 and earlier), if you wanted to search for an app, you would unlock your device, and swipe right until you got to the search screen. Now on the menu, swipe down from the middle of the menu and you'll be able to search for the app (or contact / email).

Searching on iOS 10 is a whole lot smarter. Before you even search, it will show last active apps. As you type what you are searching for, Siri begins to guess what it might be and make suggestions. It also will look deeper into apps for content — so it not only search for apps, it can search through email and documents for what you are looking for. If you have used a Macbook or iMac, it works a lot like the Finder.

Double tapping the home button, would previously bring up the apps you were using (the multitasking menu), and it would let you close them by tapping on the "X". Double tapping still brings up the last app, but to close them, you will swipe up. When you swipe up, you will see the app disappear. This looks a little different than iOS 8, but still works the same way.

The only major new app added in the past two years is Music. If you are familiar with Pandora or other music streaming services, then you'll be used to the interface; it works by playing music that sounds like music you love. So when you start it you'll type in an artist (like the Beatles); it will instantly start streaming different music by the Beatles or similar in sound to the Beatles. You can also type in a genre like Pop. To access this app, tap the "Music" app icon. The most popular station is the default Beat 1 station.

Other changes are to the apps themselves. The apps you love from Apple are still there — they've just been updated.

The camera app, for example, looks a bit different. There used to be switches for photo and video. Now there's a swipable menu bar on the bottom that says "Video / Photo / Square / Pano"; just slide your finger over the camera you want to use. "Square" is the only new option. Square is something you might like if you use Instagram, but probably won't use if you don't use it.

When you slide the camera to "Photo" you will notice the HDR option is also now on the bottom. If you aren't familiar with HDR, this is the feature that lets you take high-resolution photos.

In the bottom right corner, you will notice three circles. This lets you add different hues and saturation to your photo. So if you want to take a picture with an artistic tent / glow you now can without having to edit it in later.

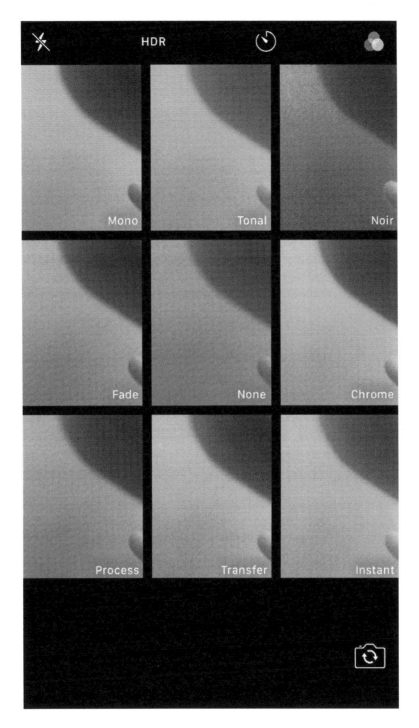

The Apple Photo app has also added a sorting system called "Collections"; you may not be aware of it, because it's a behind the scenes feature, but when you take a photo, your phone collects when it was taken (date and time) and where it was taken (the location). When you open photos and click the "Photos" tab on the bottom left of the app, your photos are initially sorted by year; click a photo within that year, and they'll be sorted by specific dates; click a photo within that collection and they'll be sorted by "Memories" or locations.

A fun newer feature of the camera app, is "Time-Lapse Photography;" time-lapses photos look kind of like animated GIFs; it's simple to use; just open the camera, and slide through the modes until you get to "Time-Lapse" and shoot the photo; you can even control exposure and set a time.

Added in iOS 10 is a folder just for selfies. Whenever you take a selfie, it is still stored in the "Photo" app, but there is a directly just for those photos.

If you are upgrading to the iPhone 6s/6s + or later then you'll take advantage of the biggest upgrade — the new iPhone has a 12MP camera (previously it was 8MP) and 4k video.

The new iPhones also have a camera feature called Live Photos; unfortunately, this is a phone feature, not a software feature — meaning if you are only updating the software (not the phone) you will not be able to take advantage of it. Live Photos is default on the camera app; whenever you take a photo, it records the seconds before and after; it does take more space, but not enough to worry about.

One of the more noticeable changes to the OS previously is in the safari app. The app is still as easy to use as it's always been, but its looks and features take a little getting used to. There's a bar on top and bottom, but when you start to scroll, you will notice the top bar gets smaller and the bottom bar goes away altogether. If you tap in the bottom of the phone (or slide your finger up or down), the bar will reappear. Not a lot has changed to Safari in iOS 10.

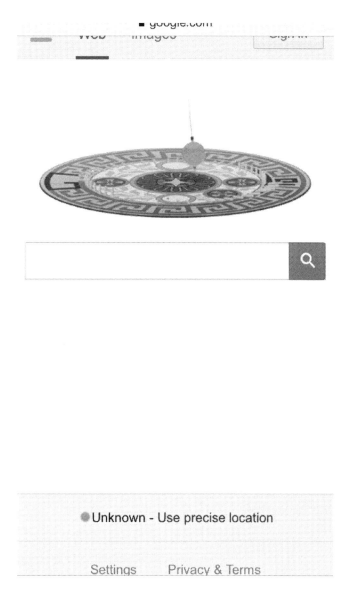

In the lower right corner, you will notice two squares; this enables a tabs feature so you can have multiple websites open.

As screens continue to grow bigger and with better resolution, it's not always necessary to see the mobile version of the website—even though that's what is displayed. Now you can see a desktop version while using Safari. Tap the address bar, scroll up and tap Request Desktop site.

One of the biggest features on the iPhone is Apple Pay, which let's you tap to pay for products (when the store supports it). In iOS 10, you can also pay online merchants (like Amazon.com) by scanning in your credit card. You must use Safari as your browser to use this feature. Apple Pays name was changed to Wallet because more store cards (not credit cards) are also being used.

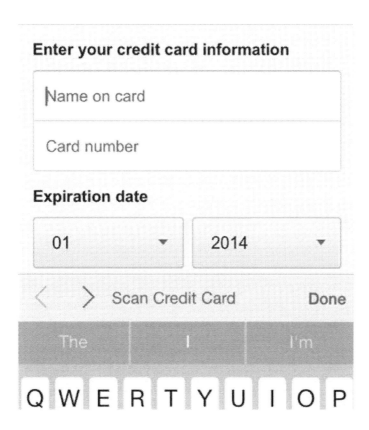

Siri has a few cosmetic and behind the hood changes; the one you will probably notice right off the bat is Siri can now have a male or female voice. To change it from female (the default voice) to male, go to Settings > General > Siri > Voice Gender.

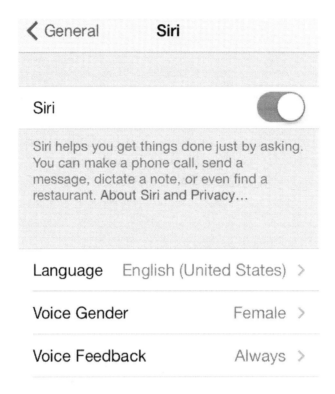

Siri can now return calls, play voicemail, search Wikipedia / Twitter, and control iTunes Radio.

Siri has been the butt of a lot of jokes over the years, but with each update she gets smarter and more responsive. With iOS 10, that's more true. She's more like a personal assistant than ever before, and can even do simple math for you. Go ahead—ask her a question and see how she responds!

For those who are upgrading from the 5, the biggest change is fingerprint recognition; if you're like my dad, then the first thing you might think is *what if someone cuts off my thumb?!* Apple actually thought of this, too! The thumb has to be living! If you're worried about privacy, the thumb print is stored locally on your phone—unlike some features (like Siri) which actually go through Apple's servers.

When the App Store is open, Siri can now search the app store for what you are looking for; just say what it is and let Siri do the rest.

We've all had this moment—we can't find our iPhone or iPad, and we ask someone to call us so we can find it; one problem…the device is dead! With iOS, when your phone gets to a critical battery levels, you can automatically send your last known location to Apple. Apple stores your last known location for 24-hours. To turn the feature on, go to Settings / iCloud / and finally Find My iPhone. From this setting you can turn it on or off.

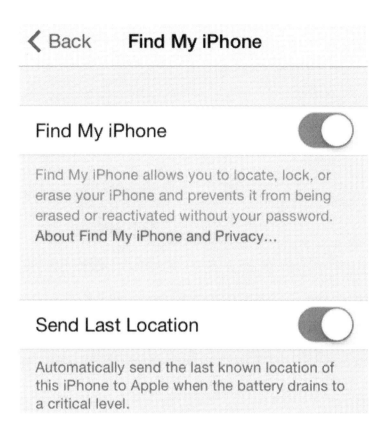

When you double tap on the Home button, your favorite contacts show up; it's faster than ever to make a phone call.

Reply to messages is a lot simpler; when you see that little notification pop up with the message, drag it down, and you will see the option to reply without opening the Message app.

Android users have long boasted about being able to add keyboards to their device; this is now a feature of the iPhone and iPad.

Spotlight (on your homescreen, drag your finger down) has always been a quick way to find contacts and apps; now you can use Spotlight to find even more—from movie show times to restaurants; it's like a mini search engine without opening up the search engine.

Group messages is a great way to text multiple people—but sometimes you want to continue a group conversion without every person in your group seeing it. Now you can remove a person from a group message exchange; just tap details and swipe to remove the person you want to take out of the conversation.

iPad users are used to being able to rotate their home screen horizontal and vertical; with new iPhones, that's now possible one newer phones.

Have you ever showed photos to family or friends and got to one that's a little…awkward? You could always delete it, but maybe it's one, as awkward as it is, that you actually want to keep? In the Photos app, tap and hold the picture you want to keep (but not show), tap "Hide." The photo will now be visible in albums, however a new "Hidden" album will be created.

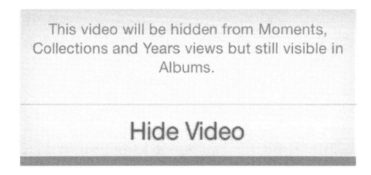

Another feature you may have heard a lot about is phone calls over Wi-Fi; while this is a powerful feature you are probably excited to use, it's not quite ready for primetime with all providers. At the initial launch of the phone, only T-Mobile has announced support of the feature.

Is your device dying faster than it should? iOS makes it a lot easier to find out what app might be running your device too hard. To see who the battery drainer is, go to Settings / General / Usage and Battery Usage.

BATTERY USAGE

Last 24 Hours	Last 7 Days

	Safari	20%
	Mailbox Background Activity	17%
	Rdio Audio	14%

Have you ever checked your device a 100 times waiting to get a reply to that important email? Let the device notify you so you don't have to keep looking down. When your Mail App is open, reply to a message, tap the flag, and tap Notify Me.

Not a good at typing text messages? When you reply to a message, tap the microphone key and send a speech message.

Having a black and white screen might help you see the screen easier; if that's true, go to Settings / Accessibility / and switch Grayscale to on.

A popular feature on the device is called HealthKit; it's Apple's way of trying to get you more active and healthy. HealthKit, at this point, is a simple tracking app—it let's you add what you ate, how you slept and how active you were. Keep an eye on this app and expect it to be enhanced and updated at some point in the future.

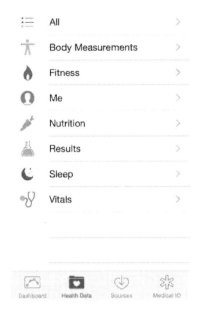

A long complaint of Apple users is how hard it is for a family to share things; Apple has heard the complaints and added Family Sharing as a feature. Family Sharing let's up to five people in your family share everything from apps to movies. The feature also let's users share billing information.

If you have all Apple products, then your life is about to get a little easier. iCloud Drive let's you share documents, videos, and other important files between devices. It's as simple as adding the document to the drive. Once that's done it shows up everywhere.

When someone calls you on iOS 10 and they are not in your contacts, your iPhone will often now take a guess about who it is based on people you have previously emailed.

The Notes app has always been the go to app for jotting down quick and simple notes—it's like Word or Pages, but without all the fancy stuff. In iOS 10, Notes is still simple—but it got a whole lot fancier…while retaining the simplicity that people love about it.

At first glance, Notes looks basically the same as it always has. Notice that little plus sign above the keyboard? That's what's different.

Tap the plus button one time, and you'll see the options that have been added.

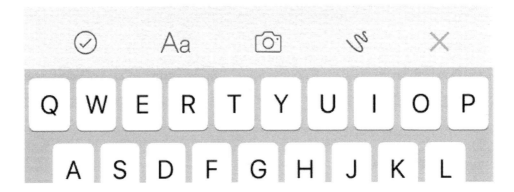

Starting from the left side is a checkmark, which is what you press if you'd like to make a checklist instead of a note. For each new checkmark, just tap the return button the keyboard.

The "Aa" button is what you would press if you would like to format the note a little (larger fonts, bold, bulleted text, etc).

The little camera button will let you add a photo you have taken or let you take a photo from within the app and insert it.

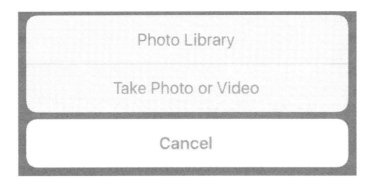

And finally the squiggly line let's you draw in the Notes app; when you press it, you'll see three different brushes (pen, marker, and pencil) that each work a little differently, as well as a ruler and eraser.

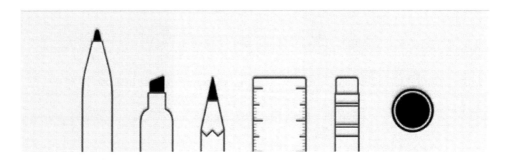

There's also a round black circle — tapping that let's you change the color of the brush.

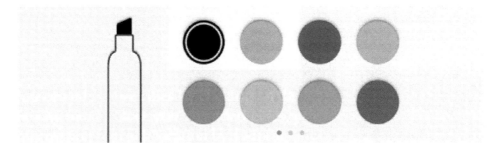

Just tap the Done button in the upper right corner once you've picked your color and it will be changed.

Once you tap the Done button after you've finished drawing, you will go back to the note. If you tap the drawing, however, it will activate it again and you can make changes or add to your drawing.

It's obviously not the most advance drawing app—but that's the point—it's not supposed to be. As the name of the app says, this app is just for jotting or drawing quick notes.

In the Settings menu a Search option has been added at the top. There's a lot of Settings in iOS and there's more and more with each update—search settings let's you quickly access the setting you want. So, for instance, if you want to stop getting notifications for a certain app, you no longer have to thumb through endless apps—now just search for it.

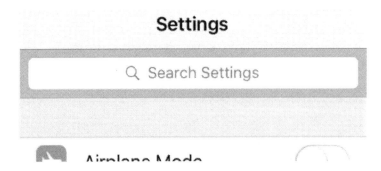

Notes has also been added to Safari, so if you want to add a website to a note, it's now possible.

There's a number of smaller changes (such as better transit guidance in Maps), which will be covered more thoroughly throughout the book.

On the device itself, the only other major feature added to new phones is 3D Touch; if you have a

MacBook or Apple Watch, you might no this as ForceTouch. ForceTouch lets you do different gestures based on how much pressure you put on the screen.

Pressing lightly on the camera app, for example, will bring up several options.

Lightly pressing on a web link lets you "peak" at the page without opening the browser to it.

Remember, this exclusive to the new iPhone so older devices won't have the option.

As you can see, there's a lot to do in iOS 10, but there's not so much that you'll be left confused and frustrated. Apple products "just work" — this is truer than ever with iOS 10. Don't be afraid to play around with the phone; there's nothing you can do to the OS to destroy it. The blue screens of death you might have once scene on old PC is not something you'll ever see on iOS. If you ever delete something on accident, it's easy to get back. Don't worry! You can do your phone no harm!

Should you upgrade to iOS if you have the older version? Absolutely! "Some" apps may not work after the upgrade — this is the only downside. As with any software update, it's up to the developers to make sure their apps are compatible — some simply do not. Major apps (like Kindle, Evernote, Dropbox) do. If you do upgrade, there is no going back! You cannot downgrade back. I recommend backing up your device before installing the update.

Can you upgrade even if you aren't getting a new iPhone or iPad? Most likely. Below is a list of compatible devices:

- iPhone (original): No

- iPhone 3G: No

- iPhone 3GS: No

- iPhone 4: No.

- iPhone 4S: No.

- iPhone 5: Yes.

- iPhone 5s: Yes.

- iPhone 5c: Yes.

- iPhone 6: Yes.

- iPhone 6 Plus: Yes.

- iPod Touch: Only the 6th-generation iPod Touch can upgrade.

- iPad (original): No

- iPad 2: No.

- iPad 3rd generation: No.

- iPad 4th generation: Yes.

- iPad Air: Yes

- iPad Mini (generation 2 and up): Yes (original, no)

Now that you've seen the new features, let's move on to a brief iPhone crash course, so you can start using it!.

The iPhone Crash Course

Now that you know a little more about the iPhone, let's see how to use it! This next section is going to walk you through everything that you need to know to get started.

Very quickly, let's first take a moment and look at your phone. There's not a lot to it: just a handful of buttons and two cameras.

On the right side of the phone is the Sleep / Wake button. Don't think of it like a power button, because you don't need to turn your iPhone on and off every time, it's always on. If you *have* to turn your phone off; you can hold down the Sleep / Wake button until the phone says "Slide to Power Off." On the bottom of the phone is your dock connector. You use this to charge your phone or plug in any extra accessories (like an iHome dock). On the left side of the phone are the volume up / down button and the Vibrate switch which by switching down your phone's ringer goes to vibrate.

On the front of the phone, right at the bottom, is the Home button. That's the button you'll be using the most, and this book will refer frequently to it. This button minimizes apps and gets you to the home screen. If you have the new iPhone 5s, then this button is replaced with the fingerprint recognition scanner. On newer phones (iPhone 7 and onward) the Home button isn't quite a button — not like it is on older phones — but it behaves in a similar way.

There are two cameras on the iPhone; one on the front (in the top center), and one on the back. The front facing camera is primarily used for Facetime and self-portraits while the back camera is usually used to take videos and photos.

So now that you know what the outside of the phone is and what it does, let's look at the meat of the phone: the software.

The first thing you will probably want to know is how to change the icons around and add your own wallpaper to make the phone more personal, and that's where we'll start. Before I show you any of this, remember that *you cannot break the iPhone software!* This isn't like old Windows computers where if you erase the wrong file you'd say goodbye to your computer! At the absolute worst, you delete something by mistake and have to download it again.

Move your finger on top of any icon, tap *and* hold it. Keep holding it for about three seconds until the icons start shaking and an 'x' appears in the upper left corner of all the apps.

Some icons cannot be deleted; these are the apps that came with the iPhone and have to stay on your phone even if you aren't using them. The ones with the 'x' can be deleted by tapping on the 'x'. A confirmation message will appear if you try to delete it by accident, so don't worry about pushing the wrong button. Even if you downloaded it, a copy of the app is stored for you, so you can re-download it again and again.

If you want to move the icons around; simply tap, hold and then drag the icon to the position you want it to be it. If you drag it all the way to the side and then keep going like if you were dragging it off the screen, a new screen appears. When you are happy with where your apps are positioned, press the Home button (remember, it's on the bottom, front, of the phone. It's the only button on the front of the phone actually). If you happened to move an icon to a new screen, you can now get to that screen by swiping or flicking your finger to the right or left depending on which screen you want to go to.

You can also put icons into folders; this is handy if you have, for instance, several game apps or reference apps. Why not group them into one place? Doing so is simple; tap and hold an app like you did before, and wait for them to start shaking with the little 'x' in the corner of them. Tap and hold the app you want to put into a folder, and then move it on top of the other app which you want to group it with. If the other app is on another screen, just drag the icon to the edge of the screen and wait for that screen to appear. You can add more icons to that group by moving them on top of the folder. When you are done, press the Home screen one time.

Now that you have your icons situated, let's change the background image of the iPhone. You can do this using one of two ways:

1. Take a picture and make it your background.
2. Find a background that you like on the Internet.

Because I am going to talk about how to use the camera app later, let's assume you want to get a photo from the Internet. I'm going to use www.google.com/images : a popular website for finding photos.

Open the Safari browser (which is on your Home screen); this is the app you will use whenever you go on the Internet.

Now that it's open, tap one time on the Address Bar (the long bar at the very top of the screen) and hit the 'x' button one time. Now type in: "google.com/images", notice how I don't type 'www'? The reason is that you don't actually need to. The iPhone is smart enough to know that you are going to a website, so it will add it in for you. When you have it typed; press 'Go' on the keyboard and the page will begin loading.

Google Images should now be on your screen. Type in something you'd want as your background. You can do this by tapping the search bar right below the Google logo it's a bit hard to see though. I'll type in "adorable puppies" because who doesn't love adorable puppies?

Now just find the image you want as your background (don't worry, you can change it later!) and tap it one time. This will bring up a larger size version of the image.

Finally, tap 'Full-Size Image' button in the upper right corner. This will make the image a little bit bigger and give us the option to save it.

When the bigger image has loaded, tap and hold the image; this brings up an option to save or copy the image. Tap the save button.

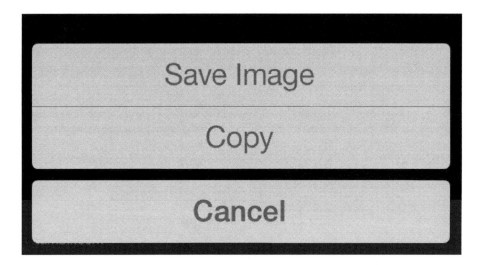

Your photo has now been saved in the 'Photos' app. This is the same place an app is stored when you take a picture with your camera.

Next press the Home button on the front of your phone to minimize. Do you notice how I say minimize? This is because technically the app is still opened in the background so you can go back to it with the multitasking feature. I'll go over that later.

From the Home screen, tap the 'Photos' icon; this will launch your photo album. From here tap the image you want to make your background.

Once it's opened, tap the button on the lower left corner with the arrow coming out of it.

This is going to bring up several options. The one we are using here is 'Use as Wallpaper.' (Note the other options, however; this is also where you would go to message, email, assign a contact photo, etc.)

Next, it will ask you to move and scale the photo. To move the photo, just tap, hold and move your finger. To scale the photo (i.e. make it bigger or larger), get two of your fingers, put them on the middle of the screen and pinch them in or out.

Once you are satisfied, tap the 'Set' button. This will bring up the options to set the image to the lock screen (when you first wake your phone up and it says 'Slide to Unlock') or to the home screen (that's the place where all of the icons are). Otherwise, you can set it to both screens. Tap the button that you want to set (remember, you can always change it).

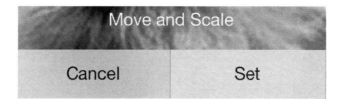

After selecting if you want it as home screen (the screen behind all your icons / apps) or as your screen photo (the first screen you see when you bring the phone on from standby mode), your phone now should have its first custom wallpaper!

Surfing the Internet with Safari

Since we've already seen how to open up the Internet browser 'Safari', let's look at that next. If you are using the iPhone, you probably already are paying for a data plan, so chances are you want to take full advantage of the Internet.

There's a good chance you are using a carrier that doesn't have unlimited web surfing. This means that if you use the Internet *a lot*, then you will have to pay extra. What I recommend is using Wi-Fi when you have it (like at home). So before we go back into 'Safari', let's look very quickly at how to enable Wi-Fi.

On your Home screen, tap the Settings icon.

The second option in the Settings menu is Wi-Fi; tap anywhere on that line once.

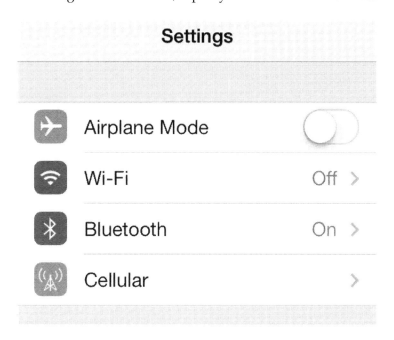

Next, switch the Wi-Fi from off to on by swiping or tapping on the 'Off'.

Your Wi-Fi network (if you have one) will now appear. Tap it once.

2WIRE103

If there is a lock next to the signal symbol; that means the Wi-Fi access is locked and you need a password to use it. When prompted, type in the password and then tap 'Join'.

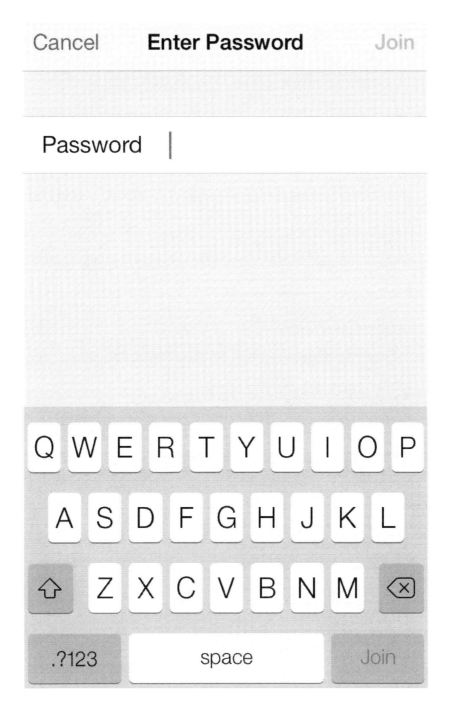

You will now connect to the network. Remember that many places, like Star Bucks, McDonalds, Nordstroms, Lowe's etc., offer free Wi-Fi as a way to entice you into the store and get you to stay. Take advantage of it and save data usage for the times you need it.

Let's see how Safari works.

Remember how I said technically you didn't close 'Safari'? Let's open it using a different way. While 'Settings' is still on your screen, press the 'Home' button twice quickly. This brings up what is called 'Multi-Tasking'. You can double tap the Home button anytime a program is open to bring up this menu. This menu allows you to quickly toggle between programs. If you've used the older iOS, then multitasking looks different. It's not little icons anymore—now you get full previews—but it still functions essentially the same. (note: if you want to close an app, swipe it down).

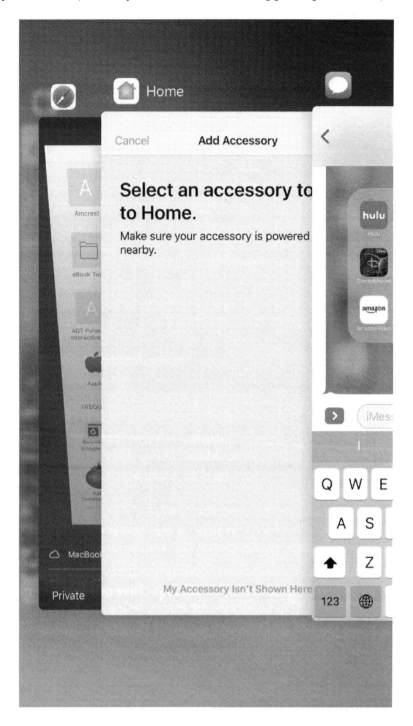

Tap the 'Safari' icon once it will launch. You've already seen how the address bar works. To search for something you use the same exact box. That's how you can search for anything on the Internet. Think of it like a Google, Bing, or Yahoo! search engine in the corner of your screen. In fact, that's exactly what it is. Because when you search, it will use one of those search engines to find results.

On the bottom of the screen you'll see five buttons; the first two are back and forward buttons that makes the website go either backwards or forwards to the website you were previously on.

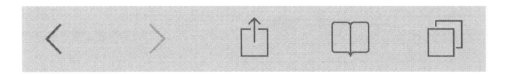

Next to the forward arrow, right in the middle, is a button that lets you share a website, add it to the 'Home Screen', print it, bookmark it, copy it, or add it to your reading list.

That's great! But what does it all mean? Let's look at each button on the menu:

1. Social Buttons: Mail, Message, Twitter, Facebook are 'Social Buttons'; pressing any of them will share the website you are looking at with whichever button you pressed (Message, FYI, is text message)
2. Add to Home Screen: If you go to a website frequently, this can be very convenient. What this button does is add an icon for that webpage right to your 'Home screen'. That way whenever you want to launch the website, you can do it directly from the 'Home screen'.
3. Print: If you have an AirPrint compatible printer, you can print a photo, document or webpage directly from your phone.
4. Copy: This copies the website address.
5. Bookmark: If you go to a website often but don't want to add it to your 'Home screen' then you can bookmark it. I will show you this in more detail in just a moment.
6. Add to Reading List: If you have a bunch of news stories open, you can add them to a Reading List to read later (even if you are offline).

The next button over, which looks like a book, is the bookmark button.

Let's go back to the bookmark button and see how that works.

When you add a bookmark (remember you do this from the previous button, the middle one), it will ask you to name it. By default it will put it in the general bookmarks tab, but you can also create new folders by clicking on 'Bookmarks'.

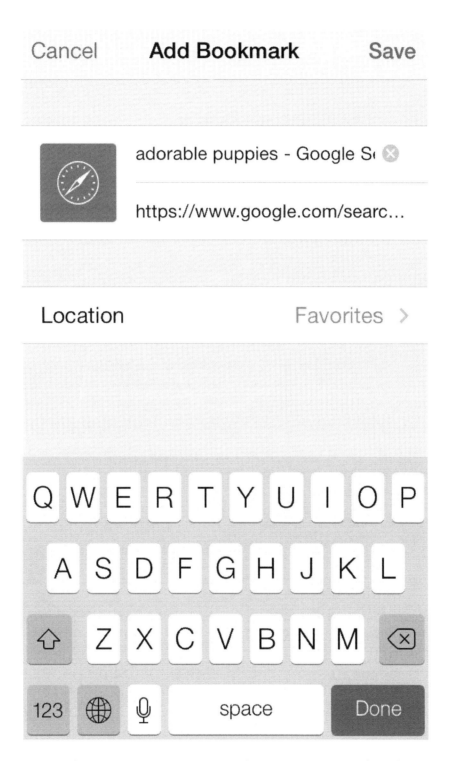

Now you can access the website anytime you want without typing the address by tapping on the Bookmarks button.

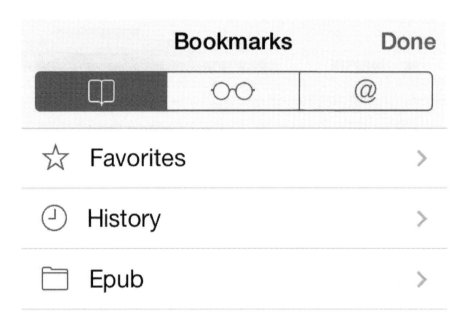

The iCloud tab is something you'll want to pay attention to if you use another Apple device (like an iPad, an iPod Touch or a Mac computer). Your safari browsing is automatically synced; so if you are browsing a page on your iPad, you can pick up where you left off on your iPhone.

The last button looks like a box on top of a transparent box.

If you use a computer or an iPad; then you probably know all about tabs. Apple decided to not use tabs on 'Safari'. Tabs are there in another way though, that's what this button is; it lets you have several windows open at the same time. When you press it, a new window appears. There's an option to open a New Page. Additionally, you can toggle between the pages that you already have opened. Hitting the red 'x' will also close a page that you have opened. Hit done to go back to normal browsing.

When you put your phone in landscape (i.e. you turn it sideways), the browser also turns and you will now have the option to use Full-Screen mode. Tap the double arrows to activate it.

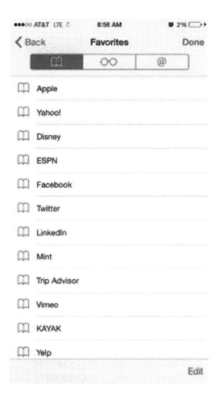

Reading list is the middle icon that looks like a pair of glasses where you can view all of the web pages, blog posts, or articles that you've saved for offline reading. To save a piece of internet literature to your reading list, tap on the Share icon and then click on Add to Reading List. Saved pages can be deleted like a text message by swiping from right to left and tapping on the red Delete button.

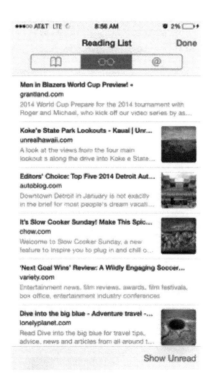

The third tab on the Bookmarks page is where you can view your shared links and subscriptions. Subscriptions can be created from any web page that provides RSS feeds, and your phone will automatically download the latest articles and posts. To subscribe to a site's RSS, visit the website, tap the Bookmark icon, and select Add to Shared Links.

Back on the main Safari home page, the last button found on the bottom right corner is Tabs. Just like the Mac version you can have multiple tabs of web pages open at the same time, and switch between them with ease. To switch the tabs into private mode where your browsing history or cookies will not be saved or recorded, tap the Tabs button and select Private. You will be asked to either close all existing tabs or keep them. If you don't want to lose any tabs that might still be open, opt to keep them. Existing tabs, in addition to any new tabs you open, will now be shielded behind private browsing.

Phone and Contacts

The iPhone lets you surf the web, edit photos, record HD videos, watch movies and you know what else? It lets you make phone calls! Of course you knew that! But for everything the iPhone does, it's sometimes easy to forget the iPhone's primary function is a phone. So let's learn how to use it!

First, tap on the Phone icon.

This launches the phone app. Notice the tabs on the bottom of the screen. Let's go over what each one does.

1. Favorites: These are the people you call most frequently. They are also in your contacts. It's kind of like your speed dial.
2. Recent: Any call (Outgoing or Incoming) will show up here. Incoming calls are in black, and outgoing calls are in red.
3. Contacts: This is where every contact will be. Do you notice the letters on the side? Tap the letter corresponding to the person you want to call to jump to that letter.
4. Keypad: This is what you use if you want to call the person using an actual keypad.
5. Voicemail: all your voicemail is stored here until you erase it.

Personally, I like to add contacts by going to icloud.com and signing in with my iTunes Account. It automatically syncs with the phone and is web-based which means that it doesn't matter whether you are using a Mac or a PC. I prefer this way because I can type with a real keyboard.

For the sake of this book, however, I am going to use the phone method; which is almost identical to the iCloud.

To add a contact, tap on 'Contacts', and then tap the '+' button in the upper right corner. Additionally, you can remove contacts by tapping on the edit button instead and then tapping on the person you want to delete, and then hitting delete.

Edit   **Favorites**   +

To insert information, all you need to do is tap in each field. If you tap on 'add photo' you will also have the option of taking someone's photo or using one you already have. If you want to assign a ringtone or a vibration, so that it plays a certain song only when this person is calling, then add that under ringtones. When you are finished, tap done. It will now give you the option of adding the person to your favorites if this is someone you will call often.

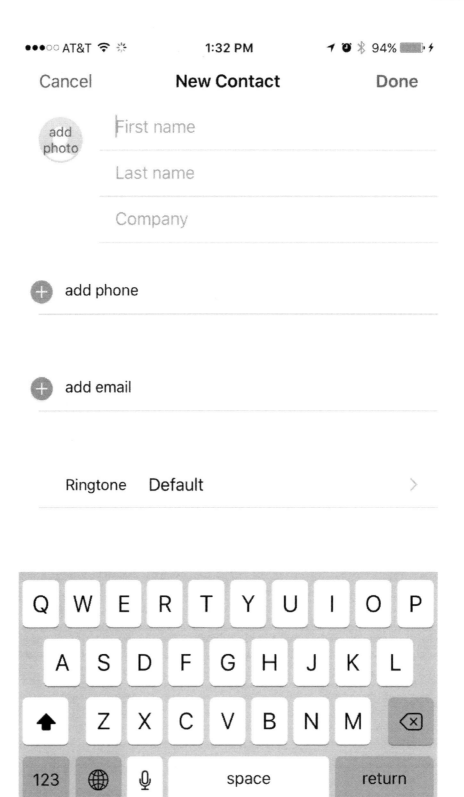

To call any person, simply tap their name. If you want to send them a text message instead, tap the blue arrow to the side of their name, note that only the blue arrow shows up if in the 'Favorites' section. To call someone not in your favorites, tap on their name in contacts and it will ask you if you want to call or text. If you prefer to call the person using Facetime (if they have Facetime) you will also have the option by tapping the blue exclamation button.

One highly advertised feature on the iPhone is 'Do Not Disturb'. When this feature is turned on, no calls get through; you don't even see that your phone ringing unless it's from someone in your approved list. That way you can have it set to ring only if someone in your family is calling. To use this feature, you need to go to your 'Settings' on your home screen.

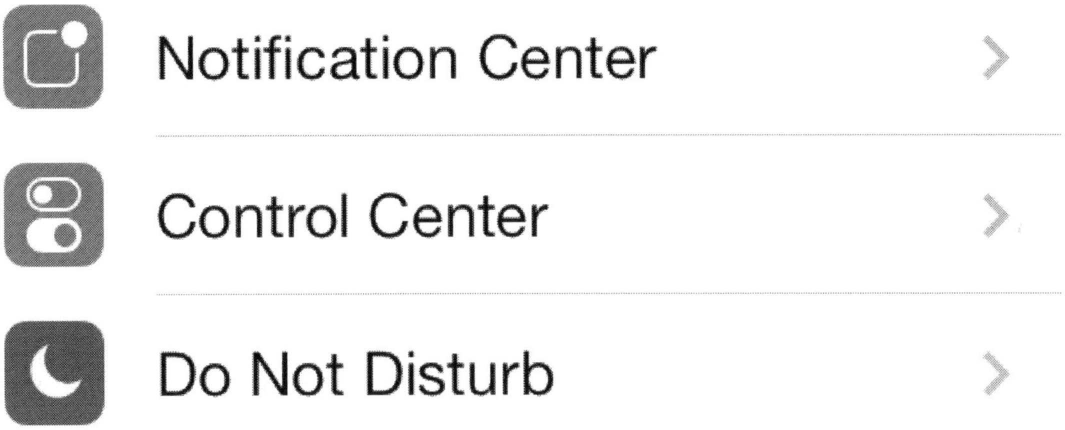

Notification Center   >

Control Center   >

Do Not Disturb   >

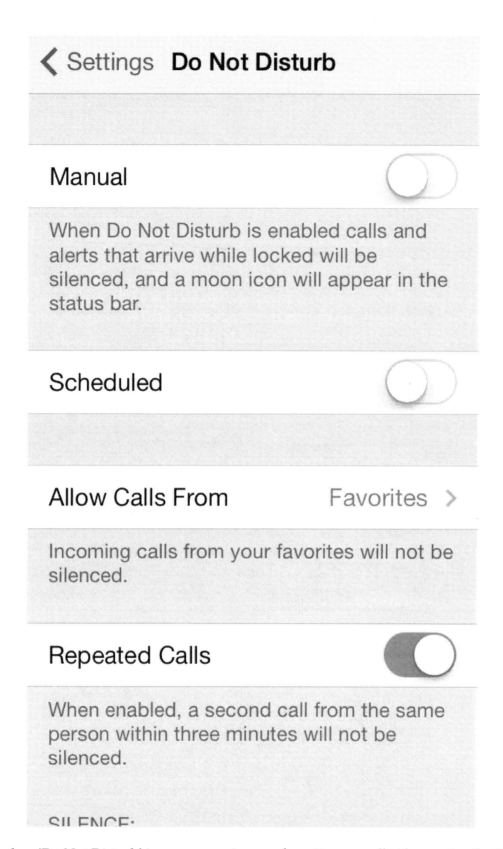

‹ Settings   Do Not Disturb

Manual

When Do Not Disturb is enabled calls and alerts that arrive while locked will be silenced, and a moon icon will appear in the status bar.

Scheduled

Allow Calls From   Favorites ›

Incoming calls from your favorites will not be silenced.

Repeated Calls

When enabled, a second call from the same person within three minutes will not be silenced.

SILENCE:

By default, when 'Do Not Disturb' is on, anyone in your favorites can call. Also, notice the 'Repeated Calls' button which is switched on by default. What that means is that if the same person calls twice in three minutes, it will go through.

If you want to set it to let no calls go through, tap on the 'Allow Calls From'. To get back to the previous menu, just tap the 'Do Not Disturb' button in the upper left corner. Anytime you see a button like that in the upper left corner, it means that it will take you to the previous screen. The information here saves as soon as you tap it, so don't worry about a save button.

Taking Photos and Vidoes

Now that you know how to make a phone call, let's get back to the fun stuff! I'll look at using the photo app next.

The camera app is on your 'Home' screen, but you can also access it from your 'lock' screen for quick, easy access. To access it, just swipe right.

The camera app is pretty simple to use. First, you should know that the camera app has two cameras; one on the front and one on the back.

The front camera has a lower resolution and is mostly used for self-portraits; it still takes excellent photos, but just remember the back camera is better. To access it, tap the button in the top right corner (the one with the camera and two arrows). The bar on the bottom has all your camera modes. This is how you can switch from photo to video mode.

In the upper-left corner of the screen you will see a lightening button. That's your flash. Tap this button and you can toggle between different flash modes.

If you want to take higher definition photographs; (Note: all video is already HD), then you'll want to turn 'HDR' on.

The last three buttons you won't use quite as much. The first, the circle, is for live photos; live photos takes a short video while you take the photo; it's so quick you won't even know it did it; it's on automatically, so tap it once to turn it off; if you tap and hold a photo with live photo enabled, then you will see the video. Next to that is a timer, which, as you might expect, delays the shot so you can take a group photo. And finally the last button let's you add different colors to the photo.

One of the photo modes is called "Pano" or Panorama. Panorama is the ability to take an extra long photo that's over 20 megapixels in size. To use it tap the 'Panorama' button. On screen instructions will now appear. Simply press the 'Shoot' button at the bottom of the screen, and rotate the camera as straight as possible while following the line. When it reaches the end, the photo will automatically go into your album.

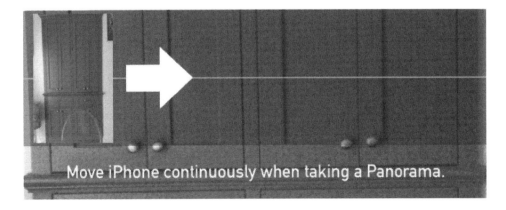

As you've probably heard, the new iPhone 7 Plus has a new and improved camera—two lenses as a matter of fact! What does that mean for how you use the camera? Not a whole lot. The change is mostly internal and seamless, which means you are getting sharper, more colorful photos, without doing anything. One thing you can take advantage of, however, is the new optical zoom on the iPhone 7 Plus; to use it, just tap the number 1 at the center of the screen, and hold it as you swipe to the left; you can also zoom the old fashion way by pinching your fingers on the screen. Once you want to unzoom, just tap on the circle with the number to reset.

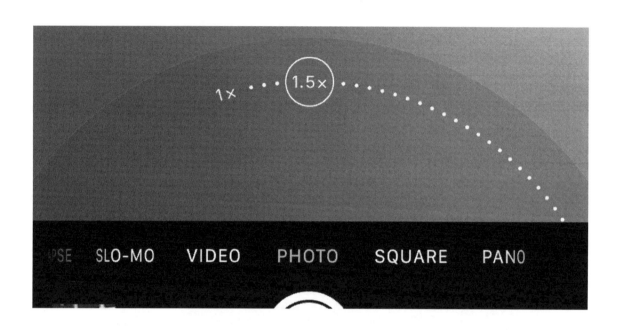

Photo Editing

Editing your photos is just as easy as taking them. As simple as editing tools are, they are also quite powerful. If you want more power though, you can always download one of the hundreds of photo editing apps in the app store.

To edit a photo, tap the 'Photo' icon on your 'Home' screen.

When you launch 'Photos', you will see a tab with three buttons; right now, I'll be talking about the 'Photos button, but we'll talk about 'Photo Stream' in the next chapter. Tap albums and let's get editing!

Next, tap the photo you want to edit and then tap 'edit' in the upper-right corner. This will open the editing menu. On the bottom of the screen, you will see all the options: undo, auto correct (which corrects the color of the photo), color change, red eye removal, and finally crop.

The only added feature is the middle one, which let's you change the color saturation.

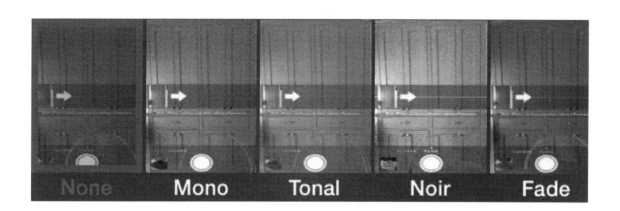

When you are satisfied with the changes tap save in the upper right corner.

Remember whenever you want to get to the previous screen just tap the back button in the upper-left corner.

Photo Albums and Photo Sharing

So now that your photo is taken and edited, let's see how to share photos.

There are several ways to share photos. When you open a photo, you will see an option bar on the bottom. The older version had more options—these options have now been moved to one central place, which you will see next.

The first button lets you share the photo socially and to media devices..

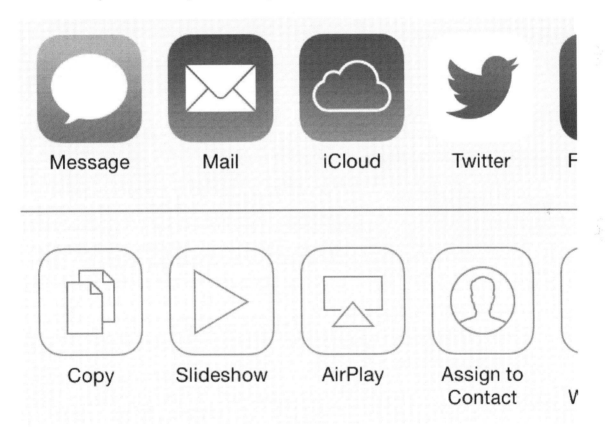

The top row is more of the social options; the bottom row is more of the media options. AirPlay, for example, let's you wirelessly send the photos if you have an Apple TV.

Finally, the last button lets you delete the photo, don't worry about accidently deleting a photo, because it ask you to confirm if you want to delete the photo before you delete it.

Next, let's go to the middle tab. 'Photo Stream' is sort of like 'Flickr'; it lets you share your photos with your family and friends easily. To get 'Photo Stream', tap the 'Shared button on the bottom of the photo app.

On the top left corner is a '+' sign; tap it.

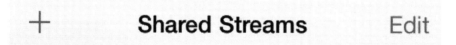

This brings up a menu that lets you create a shared directory. From there you can choose the name, who sees it and if it's a public or private photo stream. To choose a person in your contacts tap the blue '+' sign.

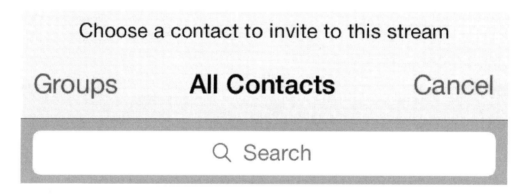

Once the album is created, tap the plus sign and tap on each photo you want to add, then hit done.

Once your family or friend accepts your 'Stream' invitation, you will automatically begin syncing your photos. Anytime you add a photo to your album, they will receive a notification.

The new iOS will now also group your photos as memories; it does this by looking at where the photo was taken and when it was taken. So you'll start noticing groups like "Christmas Memories."

Buying and Removing Apps

I mentioned there being lots of photo editing apps. So how do you buy, download and finally remove apps? I'll look at that in this section.

To purchase apps, and I don't actually mean paying for them because you can buy a free app without paying for it, follow the following:

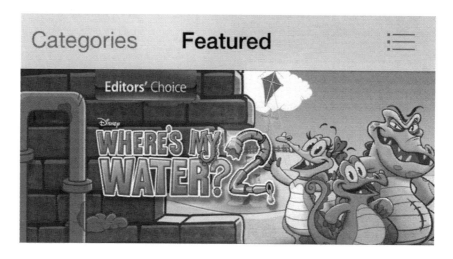

New & Noteworthy

See All >

Where's My Water? 2
Games
FREE

Reeder 2
News
$4.99

Boom! Tanks
Games
FREE

Dire(
Pho
FRE

Featured   Top Charts   Near Me   Search   Updates

The first thing you see when you open the app store are the feature apps. This is to say games, lots and lots of games! Games are the top telling category in the app store, but don't worry, there is more there than just games. Later in this handbook, I will tell you some of the essential apps you should get, but for now, let's see how the app store works so that you discover some of them yourself.

In the top left corner of both the 'featured' page and the 'top charts' (to get to the top charts, tap on the button on the bottom) is a button that says 'Categories'. This is how you can break down the apps into non-game categories.

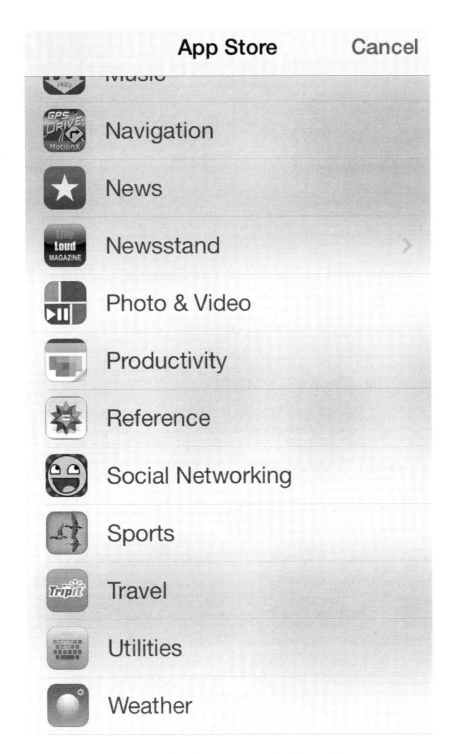

If you hear about a new app and want to check it out, use the 'Search' option.

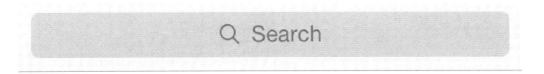

When you find an app you want to buy, simply tap the price button and type in your App store password. Remember that just because an app is free to download doesn't mean you won't have to pay something to use it. Many apps use 'in-app purchases' which means that you have to buy something within the app. You will be notified before you purchase anything though.

Apps are constantly coming out with updates like new, better features. Updates are almost always free, unless noted, and are easy to install. Just click on the last tab: 'updates'. If you have any apps that need to be updated, you will see it here. You will also see what's new in the app. If you see one, tap 'update' to begin the update.

If you bought an app, but accidently deleted it, or changed your mind about deleting it, don't worry! You can download the app again in the same place that you see the updates. Just tap on 'Purchased'.

When you tap the 'Purchased' button, you will see two options: one is to see all the apps you have purchased and one to just see the apps that you have purchased but are not on your phone. Tap the one that says 'Not on This iPhone' to re-download anything, at no cost. Just tap the Cloud button to the right of the screen. You can even download it again if you bought it on another iPhone as long as it's under the same account.

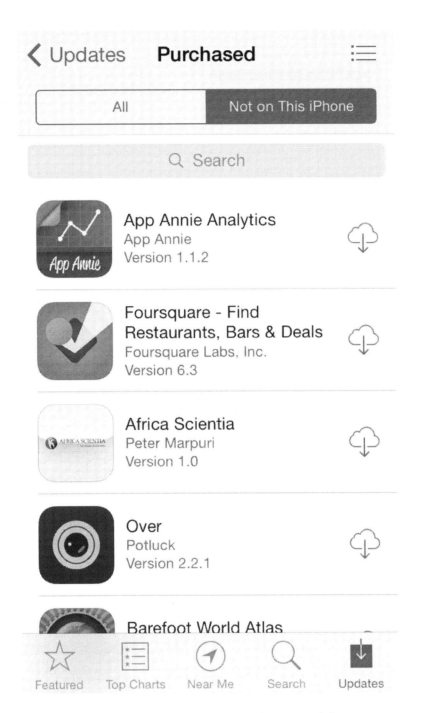

Deleting apps is easy; on your 'home' screen, tap and hold the icon of the app you want to remove, then tap the 'x' on top of the app.

Siri

By now, you probably know all about Siri and how it can remind you of things. If not, press and hold the bottom, square, button on the iPhone to activate it.

So what exactly do you do with it? The first thing you should do is introduce Siri to your family. Siri is pretty smart, and she wants to meet your family. To introduce her to your family, activate Siri by pressing and holding the 'Home' button and say: "Brian is my brother" or "Susan is my boss." Once you confirm the relationship you can now say things like: "Call my brother" or "email my boss."

Siri is also location-based. What does that mean? It means that instead of saying: "Remind me to call wife at 8 am" you can say: "Remind me when I leave work to call wife" and as soon as you step out of the office you will receive a reminder. Siri can be a bit frustrating at first, but it's one of the phone's most powerful apps, so give it a chance!

Everyone hates dealing with waits. There's nothing worse than being hungry and having to wait an hour for a table. Siri does her best to make your life easier by making reservations for you. For this to work, you'll need a free app called 'OpenTable' (you'll also need a free account), which is in the 'Apple App store'. This app makes its money by restaurants paying it, so don't worry about having to pay to use it. Once it's installed, you will simply activate Siri (press the Home button until it turns on) and say: "Siri, make me a reservation at the Olive Garden", (or wherever you want to eat). Note that not all restaurants participate in 'OpenTable', but hundreds (if not thousands) do, and it's growing monthly, so if it's not there, it probably will be soon.

Siri is ever evolving. And with the latest update, Apple has taught her everything she needs to know about sports. Go ahead, try it! Press and hold the 'Home' button to activate Siri, and then say something like: "What's the score in the Kings game" or: "Who leads the league in homeruns?"

Siri has also got a little wiser in movies. You can say: "Movies directed by Peter Jackson" and it will give you a list and let you see a synopsis, the review rating from 'Rotten Tomatoes', and in some cases even a trailer or an option to buy the movie. You can also say: "Movie show times" and a little of nearby movies playing will appear. At this time, you cannot buy tickets to the movie, though one can imagine that option will be coming very soon.

Finally, Siri, can open apps for you. If you want to open an app, simply say: "Open and the apps name."

Messaging

More and more smartphone users are staying connected through text messages instead of phone calls, and the iPhone makes it easy to keep in touch with everyone. In addition to sending regular SMS text messages and multimedia messages (pictures, links, video clips and voice notes), you can also use iMessage to interact with other Apple users. This feature allows you to send instant messages to anyone signed into a Mac running OS X Mountain Lion or higher, or any iOS device running iOS 5 or greater. iMessage for iOS 10 has been completely changed to make everything just a little more...animated.

On the main Messages screen you will be able to see the many different conversations you have going on. You can also delete conversations by swiping from right to left on the conversation you'd like, and tapping the red delete button. New conversations or existing conversations with new messages will be highlighted with a big blue dot next to it, and the Message icon will have a badge displaying the number of unread messages you have, similar to the Mail and Phone icons.

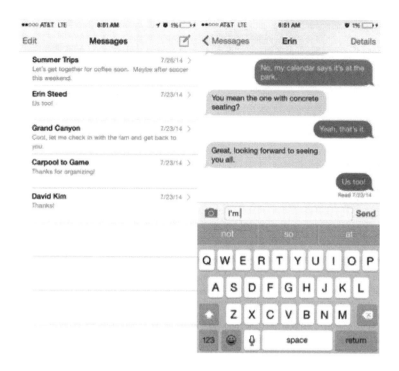

To create a message, click on the Messages icon, then the Compose button in the top right corner.

Once the new message dialog box pops up, click on the plus icon to choose from your contacts list, or just type in the phone number of the person you wish to text. For group messages, just keep adding as many people as you'd like. Finally, click on the bottom field to begin typing your message.

iMessage has a lot of new features. If all you want to do is send a message, then just tap the blue up arrow.

But you can do so much more than just send a message! (Please note, if you are sending a message with newer features to someone with an older OS or a non-Apple device, then it won't look as it appears on your screen).

To start with, go ahead and push (but don't release that blue button—or if you are using a phone with 3D Touch, press down a little firmer). This will bring up several different animations for the message.

On the top of this screen, you'll also notice two tabs; one says "Bubble" and the other says "Screen"; if you tap "Screen" you can add animations to the entire screen. Swipe right and left to see each new animation.

When you get a message that you like and you want to respond to it, you can tap and hold your finger over the message or image; this will bring up different ways you can react.

Once you make your choice, the person on the receiving end will see how you responded.

If you'd like to add animation, a photo, a video, or lots of other things, then tap the arrow next to the message.

This brings up three more options.

The first is a camera. With the camera app, you can either take a photo and send it (the first window on the left), or you can thumb through recent photos and send those instead.

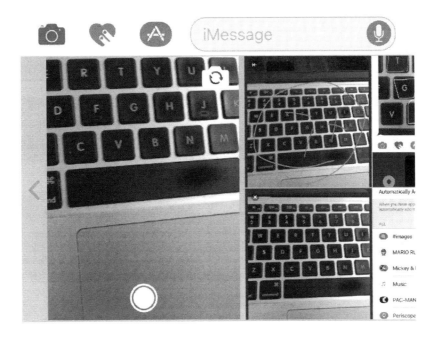

The heart with the fingers, let's you send something more personal—a drawing, a tap, or even digital kiss.

Finally, the last option is apps. You should know all about phone apps by now, but now there's a new set of apps called iMessage apps. These apps let you be both silly (send digital stickers) or serious (send cash to someone via text). To get started, tap the plus sign to open the message app store.

You can browse all the apps just like you would the regular app store. Installing them is the same as well.

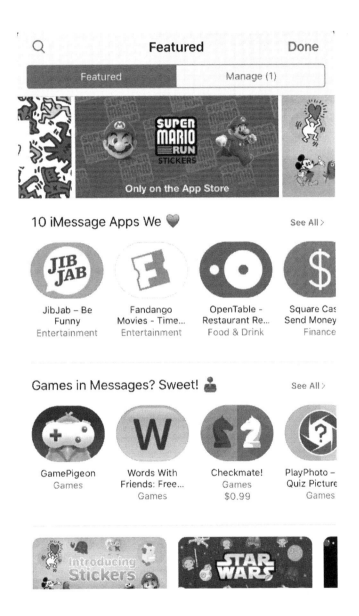

When your ready to use the app, just tap apps, tap the app you want to load, and tap what you want to send. You can also drag stickers on top of messages. Just tap, hold and drag.

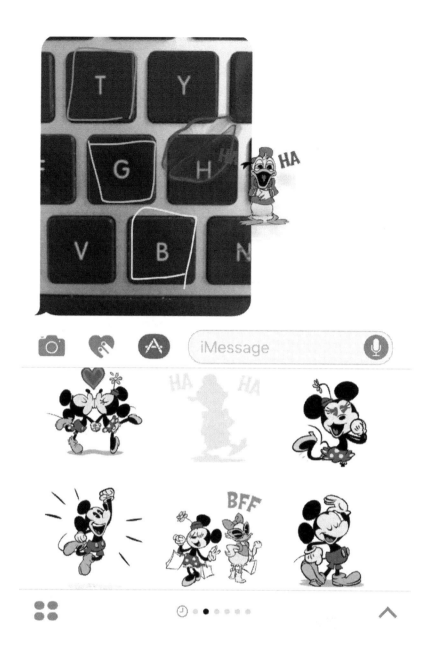

Also in the app section is a button called #images.

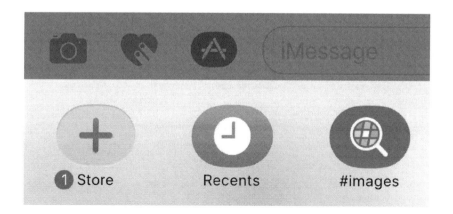

If you tap on this button you can search for thousands of humorous meme's and animated GIFs. Just tap it and search a term you want to find—such as "Money" or "Fight".

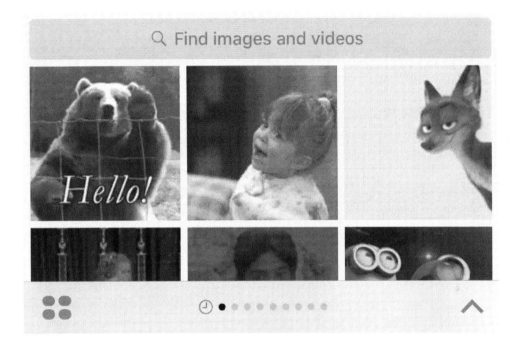

One final iMessage feature worth trying out is the personal handwritten note. Tap on a new message like you are going to start typing a new message; now rotate your phone horizontal. This brings up an option to use your finger to create a handwritten note. Sign away, and then hit done when you're finished.

happy birthday | Love You | hello | thank you | happy birthday | congratulations | th

Calendar

Among the other pre-installed apps that came with your new iPhone, perhaps one of the most used apps you'll encounter is the calendar. You can switch between viewing appointments, tasks, or everything laid out in a one day, one week, or one month view. On the iPhone 6 Plus, turn your phone on its side and you will notice everything switch to landscape mode. A first for the iPhone, many new apps now take advantage of the larger iPhone's 1080p resolution by displaying more information at once, similar to the iPad and iPad mini display. Combine your calendar with email accounts or iCloud to keep your appointments and tasks synced across all of your devices, and never miss another appointment.

Creating an Appointment

To create an appointment, click on the Calendar icon on your home screen. Click on whichever day you would like to set the appointment for, and then tap the plus sign (+) in the corner. Here you will be able to name and edit your event, as well as connect it to an email or iCloud account in order to allow for syncing.

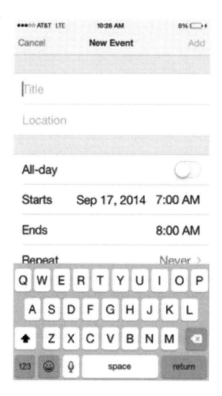

When editing your event, pay special attention to the duration of your event. Select the start and end times, or choose "All Day" if it's an all-day event. You will also have a chance to set it as a recurring event by clicking on Repeat and selecting how often you want it to repeat. In the case of a bill or car payment, for example, you could either select Monthly (on this day) or every 30 days, which are two different things. After you select your repetition, you can also choose how long you'd like for that event to repeat itself: for just one month, a year, forever, and everything in between.

Security

Entering sensitive information on websites is becoming an everyday occurrence now with the ability to shop, bank, and transfer money online. Keychain helps keep all of your usernames, passwords, and credit card information safe, but there are other precautions you can take to ensure you are protected the entire time you are surfing the web.

Phishing (pronounced "fishing") is a dangerous practice that is designed to steal a user's login information and/or credit card details. A phishing website is designed to look exactly like a trusted website (PayPal, Facebook, or your local bank for example). It's easy to not think twice about typing in your Facebook login or PayPal login information since you do it so often, but even though the website may look authentic, you might be inadvertently sending your private information to high tech thieves.

Safari comes built in with an anti-phishing setting to help protect you against sites that are known to be fraudulent or have participated in phishing activities in the past. To turn anti-phishing on, click on Settings > Safari, and toggle on Fradulent Website Warning. Now when you visit a webpage with questionable authenticity, Safari will prompt you with a warning and ask if you'd like to proceed or back out.

If you've ever returned to an online store that still had your shopping cart intact and ready to check out, you've seen cookies in action. Cookies are small bits of data that are stored on websites to provide them with more information about you. It helps websites remember stored data such as saved login information or unfinished shopping carts, but it can also help advertisers target you with specific ads based on your browsing habits. If you'd like to disable cookies, go to Settings > Safari > Block Cookies and select one of the choices. The most common choices are Always Allow, Allow from Websites I Visit (for your frequented web pages), and Always Block. Keep in mind, however, that some sites may need cookies to be enabled in order to work correctly.

Mail

The iPhone lets you add multiple email addresses from virtually any email client you can think of. Yahoo, Gmail, AOL, Exchange, Hotmail, and many more can be added to your phone so that you will be able to check your email no matter where you are. To add an email address, click on the Settings app icon, then scroll to the middle where you'll see Mail, Contacts & Calendar. You will then see logos for the biggest email providers, but if you have another type of email just click on "Other" and continue.

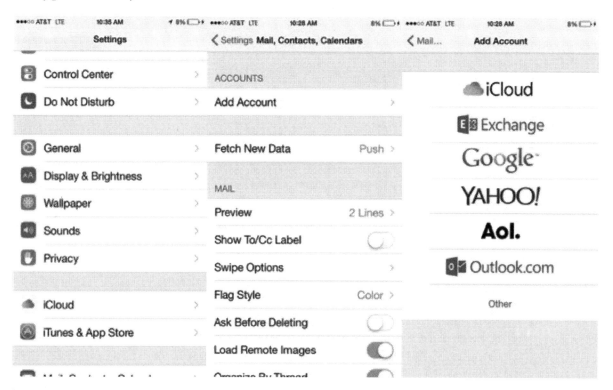

If you don't know your email settings, you will need to visit the Mail Settings Lookup page on the Apple website. There you can type in your entire email address, and the website will show you what information to type and where in order to get your email account working on the phone. The settings change with everyone, so what works for one provider may not work with another. Once you are finished adding as many email accounts as you may need, you will be able to click on the Mail app icon on your phone's home screen, and view each inbox separately, or all at once.

Maps

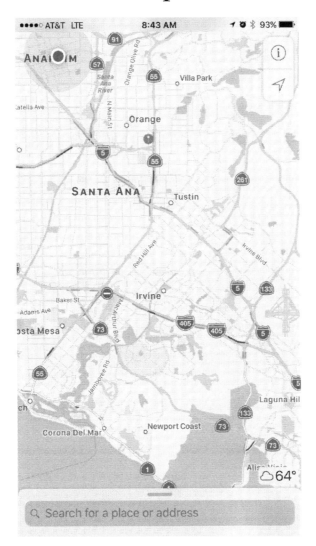

The Maps app is back and better than ever. After Apple parted ways with Google Maps several years ago, Apple decided to develop its own, made-for-iPhone map and navigation system. The result is a beautiful travel guide that takes full advantage of the newest iPhone resolutions. Full screen mode allows every corner of the phone to be filled with the app, and there's an automatic night mode just like with iBooks. You'll be able to search for places, restaurants, gas stations, concert halls, and other venues near you at any time, and turn-by-turn navigation is available for walking, biking, driving, or commuting. Traffic is updated in real time, so if an accident occurs ahead of you or there is construction going on, Maps will offer a faster alternative and warn you of the potential traffic jam.

The turn-by-turn navigation is easy to understand without being distracting, and the 3D view makes potentially difficult scenarios (like highway exits that come up abruptly) much more pleasant. Another convenient feature is the ability to avoid highways and toll roads entirely.

To set up navigation, tap on the Maps icon. On the bottom of the screen is a search for place or address; for homes you need an address, but businesses just need a name. Click on it and enter your destination once prompted.

When you find your destination's address, click on Route, and choose between walking or driving directions. For businesses, you also have the option of reading reviews and calling the company directly.

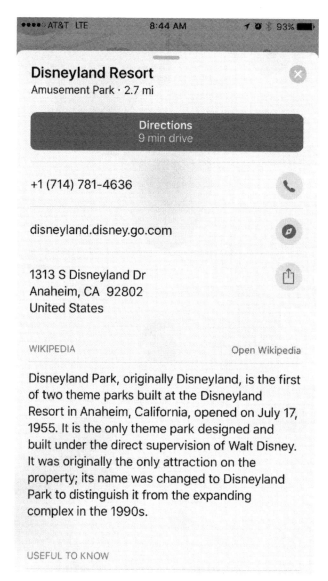

For hands-free navigation, press and hold the home button to enable Siri (which will be discussed in the next section) and say "Navigate to" or "Take me to" followed by the address or name of the location that you'd like to go to.

If you'd like to avoid highways or tolls, simply tap the more options button and select the option that you want.

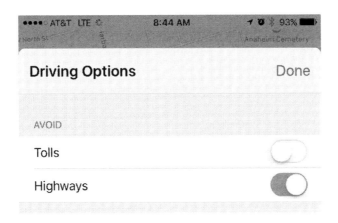

Apple Maps also let's you see a 3D view of thousands of locations. To enable this option, tap the "i" in the upper right corner. After this, select satellite view.

If 3D view is available you'll notice a change immediately. You can use two fingers to make your map more or less flat. You can also select 2D to remove 3D altogether.

Health

The release of the latest iPhone models brought with it a much greater focus on one's health, and as such, the new iPhones come with the Health app. The Health app keeps track of many different things pertaining to your health, including calories burned, your weight, heart rate, body measurements, and even an emergency card that lets you store important health information such as your blood type and allergies in the event of an emergency. There are four different tabs at the bottom of the app:

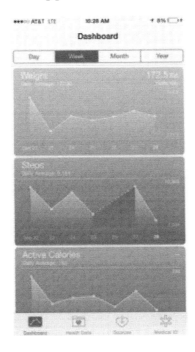

Dashboard

Here you will be able to see an at-a-glance view of your vitals, including calories burned, weight, and heart rate. You will be able to choose between one day's worth of information, a week, month, and even a year if you'd like to see how your health today compares to last year.

Health Data

This page is the main hub where you can find and store all of your information. It's broken down into a few general categories like body measurements, fitness, nutrition, sleep, and vitals, but can include even the smallest details like your blood sugar level, glucose levels, sleep patterns, current medications, and more.

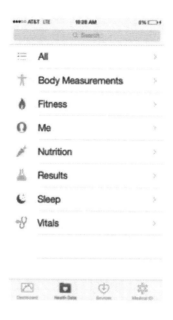

Sources

Sources weren't available at launch, but it's finally been released to much acclaim. This section is where you can control who or what can access your health information, as well as who can send you information regarding your health.

It's meant to connect to third party apps or doctors in order to send them accurate information about you, and a quick snapshot of how your days are even when you aren't visiting the doctor. This could be especially beneficial to you if you have a health condition that requires more frequent monitoring, such as diabetes.

Medical ID

Here is the virtual emergency card we mentioned earlier. This is the place to store all the important information about you in case a medical worker needs it in the event of an emergency. Enter in your blood type, allergies (medical or otherwise), chronic health conditions, diseases, medications, emergency contact, and anything else you can think of so whoever is treating you can access revenant information without wasting time.

Medical Conditions

Hypertension

Medical Notes

In case of emergency, please call Chloe Appleseed and Dr. Michael O'Reilly.

Allergies & Reactions

Penicillin - Severe skin rash

Medications

Lisinopril (10mg by mouth once a day)
Hydrochlorothiazide (12.5mg by mouth once a day)

Updated on Sep 28, 2014, 10:28 AM

Dashboard   Health Data   Sources   Medical ID

Apple Stores

iBooks

Now that the iPhone features bigger screens (iPhone 6 and up), you can probably do more and more reading on your phone while reading less on your iPad. If that's the case, you will love the new version of iBooks. Your favorite books can be read in complete full screen mode, and flick through the pages to enjoy that classic page-turning animation. Trying to organize your library and keep track of which books you have left to complete a book series? Now iBooks automatically sorts books by series, keeping everything neat and tidy for you.

The latest updates enable you to upload quotes directly to your favorite social networking or blogging site, and if you see a word you aren't familiar with, just press and hold it until the word in question becomes highlighted, then select Dictionary. Additionally, night time reading has gotten easier with the night theme. Dim or shut the lights off while reading and iBooks will automatically switch to night mode for easier viewing. Turn the lights back on, and the theme will switch back to normal reading mode.

App Store

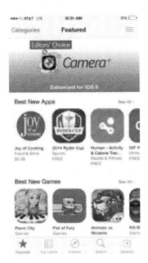

The App Store - the iPhone's meat and potatoes. Here you will be able to add as much functionality as you can possibly think of to your phone. Need a maritime GPS, restaurant manager, CRM tracker, or an accounting app? These and many, many more can be found in the App Store, where over 1.3 million apps are waiting to be explored with more added each and every day.

You can sort through the options by category (including business, finance, education, reference, games, and productivity), top free, top paid, and editor's picks. Of course, if you'd prefer to just search for whatever comes to mind, you can also select the search icon on the bottom tray or the magnifying glass in the upper right corner to search for particular titles.

At the end of this guide, we provide you with a comprehensive list of the top 25 free apps, as well as the top 25 paid apps to get you started.

iTunes

The iTunes app found on your home screen opens the biggest digital music store in the world. You will be able to purchase and download not just music, but also countless movies, TV shows, audiobooks, and more. On the iTunes home page you can also find a What's Hot section, collections of music, and new releases.

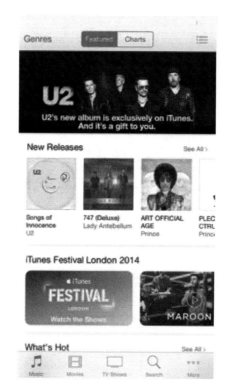

At the top you will see the option to view either featured media, or browse through the top charts. On the upper left corner is the Genres button. Clicking Genres will bring up many different types of music to help refine your search.

When you find a song, album, or movie that you want to download, you will be greeted with a screen displaying information such as ratings, reviews, related, a track list, short description, and the price.

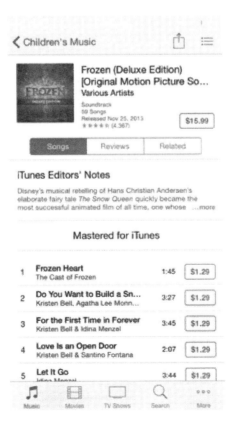

If you already have iTunes on your Mac or PC, you can sync your iPhone with it by connecting through Wi-Fi or a USB cable. If you have iTunes automatically sync with devices any time you plug them in, no further steps are necessary. If not, you can connect wirelessly by having both devices on the same Wi-Fi network. On the computer, go to iTunes, find your phone's name, select Summary, and then Sync with this iPhone over Wi-Fi. For this feature to work though, your iPhone needs to be plugged into a power source until the sync is complete.

To physically connect the two devices, plug your phone into the computer using the USB sync cable that came with the iPhone, and wait for your phone's name to come up on the computer screen. Once it does you will be able to choose between a few different options including automatically sync every time the iPhone is connected to iTunes, or choose just a few categories to sync like music or photos. Contacts and calendars used to be synced through iTunes, but today they are typically backed up through iCloud instead. Syncing contacts even when they are stored on iCloud could result in doubles of every contact you have stored.

Weather

You can use your iPhone's location services and GPS to help you navigate to your destinations, but other apps can use it to display localized information. The Weather app is one such example of this. Opening it up will immediately show you basic weather information based on your current location. To get more detailed information, you can swipe left and right on the middle section to scroll through the hourly forecast, and swipe up and down on the bottom section to scroll through the 10 day forecast.

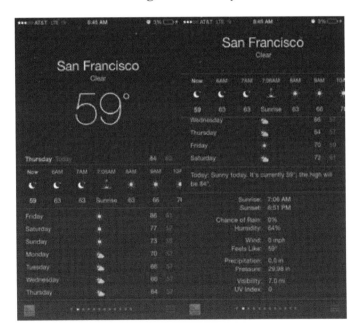

You can add more cities by clicking on the list icon towards the bottom right and searching for the city name. Once you've added cities, you can scroll between cities to see real-time weather information for each location by swiping left or right, and the number of cities you have added are shown at the bottom in the form of small dots.

94

Accessibility

The iPhone is designed to be enjoyed by everyone, and comes with several different features to allow users with disabilities to use the phone easier.

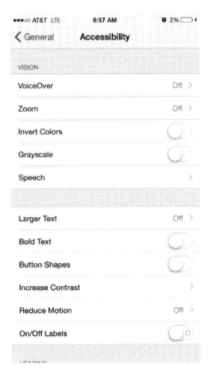

Zoom

The Zoom feature itself is not new, but iOS 8 tweaks Zoom and provides more robust tools for controlling it where and when you want it. Now you'll be able to zoom the keyboard, have the zoom follow wherever you are focused, and blow up a portion of the screen between 1000-1500 percent while keeping the rest of the screen in its native size.

Text

If you have a tough time viewing the on-screen text or just want to avoid unnecessary eye fatigue, you can enlarge the font by going to Settings > Accessibility > Larger Type and toggling on Larger Dynamic Type. At the bottom, you will also be able to drag a slider indicating how large you'd like the font on the phone to be. Maybe the font is large enough, but you need it to be heavier in order to increase legibility. If that's the case, go to Settings > General > Accessibility and toggle Bold Text. You will need to reboot your iPhone for the changes to take complete effect.

If you prefer the phone to have darker colors overall, you can invert the colors by going to

Settings > General > Accessibility and toggling Invert Colors on or off.

VoiceOver

Those with significant visual impairment will benefit from using VoiceOver, a built-in system that will speak out every single action and menu item that you touch, including scrolling and clicking links. It can be activated by rapidly clicking the home button three times, or going to Settings > General > Accessibility > VoiceOver and toggling between on and off. Also in this menu you will find options for speaking rate, hints, sound effects, and pitch change to shake off that robotic voice you may remember.

Security

Passcode (dos and don'ts, tips, etc.)

In this day and age, it's important to keep your device secure. You may or may not want to set up a touch ID (you will read more about it next), but at the very least it's a good idea to maintain a passcode. Anytime your phone is unlocked, restarted, updated, or erased, it will require a passcode before allowing entry into the phone. To set up a passcode for your iPhone, go to Settings > Passcode, and click on Turn Passcode On. You will be prompted to enter a 4 digit passcode, then re-enter to confirm. Here are a few tips to follow for maximum security:

Do's

DO create a unique passcode that only you would know

DO change it every now and then to keep it unknown

DO select a passcode that can be easily modified later when it's time to change passcodes

Don'ts

DON'T use a simple passcode like 1234 or 5678

DON'T use your birthday or birth year

DON'T use a passcode someone else might have (for example, a shared debit card pin)

DON'T go right down the middle (2580) or sides (1470 or 3690)

Touch ID

Your iPhone 6 comes with a fingerprint scanner called Touch ID that allows you to unlock your phone, activate Apple Pay, make purchases in the App Store, iTunes, or iBooks, and verify yourself with just the tap of a button. To set up a fingerprint or two (you're allowed to store several), go to Settings > Passcode > Touch ID and enable it. Then select Add a Fingerprint. You will be brought to a screen prompting you to place your finger (don't click!) on the home button. It's important to hold the phone as you normally would, otherwise you run the risk of storing incorrect or distorted fingerprints.

Once the phone is comfortable in your hand, place the finger that you'd like to store on the home button, careful once again not to click it. You will see the gray fingerprint image on the screen start to fill up with pink. Remove your finger, and gently place it down again, with small variations on your placement.

Repeat this process until the entire fingerprint image is filled in, and you will automatically be taken to the next screen titled "Adjust your Grip". Here, you will need to add even more variations of your fingerprint in order to capture the edges of your fingerprint. Follow the same steps as the previous screen, and soon you will complete the fingerprint scanning process. To activate it, lock the screen and enter your passcode, then lock it again. After it's locked, you can unlock it with one finger by clicking the home button to turn the screen on, then gently resting your finger on the button. The fingerprint should register and the phone will unlock. The only times a passcode will still be required is when you initially set up a passcode, when you restart the phone, when you enter the Passcode settings, and when more than 48 hours have elapsed since you've unlocked the phone.

Encryption

With all of the personal and sensitive information that can be stored on iCloud, security is understandably a very real concern. Apple agrees with this, and protects your data with high level 128-bit AES encryption. Keychain, which you will learn about next, uses 256-bit AES encryption - the same level of encryption used by all of the top banks who need high levels of security for their data. According to Apple, the only things not protected with encryption through iCloud is mail (because email clients already provide their own security) and iTunes in the Cloud, since music does not contain any personal information.

Keychain

Have you logged onto a website for the first time in ages and forgot what kind of password you used? This happens to everyone; some websites require special characters or phrases, while others require small 8 character passwords. iCloud comes with a highly encrypted feature called Keychain that allows you to store passwords and login information in one place. Any of your Apple devices synced with the same iCloud account will be able to load the data from Keychain without any additional steps.

To activate and start using Keychain, simply click on Settings > iCloud and toggle Keychain on, then follow the prompts. After you've added accounts and passwords to Keychain, your Safari browser will automatically fill in fields while you remain logged into iCloud. If you are ready to checkout after doing some online shopping, for example, the credit card information will automatically pre-fill so you don't have to enter any sensitive information at all.

iCloud

To really get the full effect of Apple's carefully created ecosystem and be a part of it, you will need to create an iCloud account. Simply put, iCloud is a powerful cloud system that will seamlessly coordinate all of your important devices. The cloud can be a little difficult to understand, but the best way to think about it is like a storage unit that lives in a secure part of the internet. You are allocated a certain amount of space, and you can put the things that mean the most to you here to keep safe. In the case of iCloud, Apple gives you 5 GB for free.

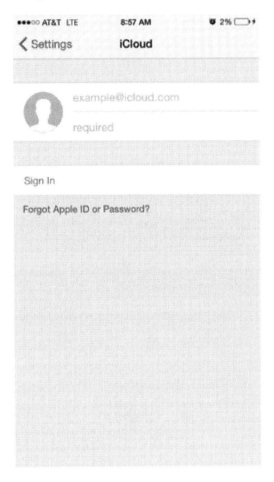

Your phone lets you automatically back up certain files such as your photos, mail, contacts, calendars, reminders, and notes. In the event that your phone is damaged beyond repair or is lost or stolen, your data will still be stored safely on iCloud. To retrieve your information, you can either log onto icloud.com on a Mac or PC, or log into your iCloud account on another iPhone to load the information onto that phone.

With the introduction of iOS 8 and the iPhone 6 and 6 Plus, Apple rolled out a few major changes. You will now be able to store even more types of documents using iCloud Drive and access them from any smartphone, tablet, or computer. Additionally, up to 6 family members will now be able to share purchases from iTunes, iBooks, and the App Store, removing the need to buy an app twice simply because you and a loved one have two different iCloud accounts.

For users who will need more than 5 GB, Apple has dramatically reduced the cost of iCloud:

- 50 GB is $0.99 per month

- 200 GB is $2.99 per month

- 1 TB (1000 GB) is $9.99 per month

- 2 TB (2000 GB) is $19.99 per month

Battery Tips

The iPhone 7 promises better battery life — the longest ever, in fact. But let's face it, no matter how great the battery is, you probably would love to have just a little bit more life in your charge.

Disable Notifications

My mom told me her battery didn't seem to be lasting very long. I looked at her phone and could not believe how many notifications were activated. She knows absolutely nothing about stocks, nor does she have any desire to learn, and yet she had stock tickers going. You might want notifications on something like Facebook, but there are probably dozens of notifications running in the background that you don't even know about, nor do you even need to. Getting rid of them is easy; Go to 'Settings', then to 'Notifications'. Anything that shows up as 'In Notification Center' is currently active on your phone. To disable them, tap on the app and then switch it to off. They aren't gone for good; anytime you want to turn them back on, just go to the very bottom where it says 'Not In Notification Center' and switch them back on.

Brightness

Turning down the brightness just a shade can do wonders for your phone and might even give your eyes some needed relief. It's easy to do; Go to 'Settings', then to 'brightness'. Just move the slider to a 'setting' that you feel comfortable with.

Email

I prefer to know when I get email as soon as it comes. By doing this, my phone is constantly refreshing email to see if anything has come in; this drains the battery, but not too terribly. If you are the kind of person who doesn't really care when they get email, then it might be good to just switch it from automatic to manual. That way it only checks email when you tap the mail button. To switch manual on, go to 'Settings', then to 'Mail, Contacts, Calendars' and finally go to 'Fetch New Data'. Now go to the bottom and tap 'Manually' (you can always switch it back later).

Location, Location, Lo…Battery Hog

Have you heard of location-based apps? These apps use your location to determine where you are exactly. It's actually a great feature if you are using a map of some sort. So let's say you are looking for somewhere to eat and you have an app that recommends restaurants, it uses your GPS to determine your location so it can tell what's nearby. That is great for some apps, but it is not so for others. Anytime you use GPS, it's going to drain your battery, so it's a good idea to see what apps are using it and question if you really want them to. Additionally, you can turn it off completely and switch it on only when needed. To do either, go to 'Settings', then to 'Location Services', switch any app you don't want to use this service to off (you can always switch it back on later).

Accessorize

90% of you will probably be completely content with these fixes and happy with their battery life; but if you still want more, consider buying a batter pack. Battery packs do make your phone a bit more bulky (they slide on and attach to the back of your phone), but they also give you several more hours of life. They cost around $70. Additionally, you can get an external battery charger to slip in your purse or briefcase These packs let you charge any USB device (including iPhones and iPads). External battery chargers cost about the same, the one advantage of a charger versus' a pack is it will charge any device that has a USB, not just the iPhone.

The easiest way to save battery life, however, is to go to Settings > Battery and switch on "Low Power Mode". This is not the ideal setting for normal phone use, but if you only have 20% of your battery and need it to last longer, then it's there.

Essential Apps

This list is not going to be full of apps you have heard of. Do you really want me to tell you about a little game called 'Angry Birds'? Or a social networking site called 'Facebook'? If you don't know about the apps, I'm sure someone in your family will tell you all about them as soon as you show them your iPhone. What follows are a few apps you might not know about, but will almost certainly benefit from. Please note that prices are set by the app publishers and may increase or decrease when you look them up.

SignNow: Free

Have you ever received an email with an attachment that needed to be signed? You print it, then scan it, then send it back. SignNow takes away some of those steps; the app lets you sign a document straight from your phone without the need to print and sign manually.

JotNot: Free. Pro Version: $1.99

Speaking of scanning, 'JotNot' lets you scan a document with your camera. You'll be surprised by the quality of the final document too. It's not the same as scanning, but it's as good as you'll get from a phone.

Google Translate: Free

This app is a travelers' dream. You can speak a word into the translator, and it will tell you how to say it in over two dozen languages. It even pronounces it for you!

SwipeSpeare – Modern Shakespeare: Free

This is a very cool Shakespeare reader. It let's you toggle between the original Shakespeare language and a modern Shakespeare language with the swipe of your finger.

Hipstamatic: Free

You'll quickly discover that there are a lot of camera apps out there. If you are a fan of vintage, then try 'Hipstamatic's app. It will turn your iPhone into a digital antique!

8mm: $1.99

8mm is the same concept as 'Hipstamatic', but instead of taking pictures with old photo cameras, it takes videos with old video cameras.

LoMeIn Ignition: $29.99

Thirty dollars is pretty steep for an app, it's the most you will probably ever pay for an app, so what makes it so great? It can log into your computer remotely from your phone. That means if you are at work and forgot a file on your computer, you can log in and email it to yourself.

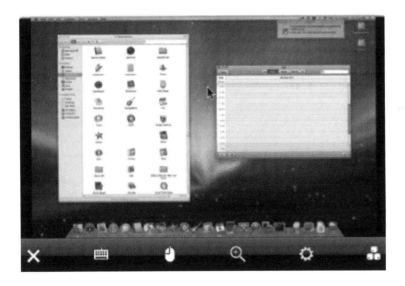

Crackle: Free

If you are a fan of 'Hulu' (the Internet website that lets you stream TV shows and movie for free), but you don't want to pay extra to get 'Hulu+' on your phone, then try 'Crackle'. It has plenty of full-length free shows like 'Seinfeld' and even has free movies.

Flixster: Free

If you go to the movies often, then this is a must have app. It gives you the show times for any movie theater near you using your phone's GPS. Several theaters also let you buy movie tickets directly from the app.

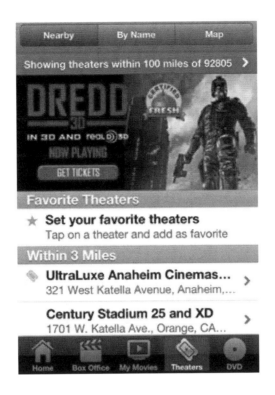

Carcassonne: 9.99

This will probably be the most expensive game you purchase on the iPhone, but it's very much worth it. If you have never played the original strategy board game then you are in for a treat. It's also great if you want to play with others who have an iPhone or an iPad.

Made in the USA
Middletown, DE
22 December 2016